WELCOME TO MIDLAND

WELCOME

to

MIDLAND

POEMS

Logen Cure

Illustrated by Ashley Shea Henderson

DEEP VELLUM PUBLISHING
DALLAS, TEXAS

Deep Vellum Publishing
3000 Commerce St., Dallas,Texas 75226
deepvellum.org · @deepvellum

Deep Vellum is a 501c3 nonprofit literary arts organization founded in 2013
with the mission to bring the world into conversation through literature.

Support for this publication has been provided in part by grants from the
National Endowment for the Arts, the Texas Commission on the Arts, the
City of Dallas Office of Arts and Culture's ArtsActivate program, and the
Moody Fund for the Arts:

ISBNs: 978-1-64605-069-7 (paperback) | 978-1-64605-070-3 (ebook)

LIBRARY OF CONGRESS CONTROL NUMBER: 2021939712

Cover art by Ashley Shea Henderson
Cover design by Justin Childress | justinchildress.co
Interior Layout and Typesetting by KGT

PRINTED IN THE UNITED STATES OF AMERICA

For Ashley

Contents

III.

IV.

Table of Illustrations

Welcome to Midland

This is a town where the roads end.
Over the wall at the end of my alley,
nothing but mesquite brush and horizon.

Dirt fills the sky, advances
a colossal wave, black blizzard,
tripping streetlights midafternoon.
Mother would stand arms akimbo
squinting out the back door,
Looks like Lubbock blowing in.

Folks would say we might just
dry up and blow away.
Bust followed that 80s boom:
half the Tall City's downtown
vacant skyscrapers haunting
vast empty parking lots,
deserted mall storefronts,
endless musak drifting
the row of locked-down security doors.

It'll turn around, they'd say. *Always does.*
Oil is king and football, crown prince.
Even when times are hard
those Robert E. Lee Rebels are champs.

Somebody's always saying
it's a great place to raise children.
People around here, they've got
character. They say
pledge allegiance under God
and mean it.

If you count yourself
a patriot, a good Christian, well,
don't be afraid
to be neighborly.

I

Permian Sea

My father told me
once all this desert was vast inland sea:
all mollusks and trilobites,
amphibians bigger than my imagination.
He pointed westward,
explained the Guadalupe Mountains
are an enormous ancient reef.
All this, he said,
everything was water.

Then the sea stagnated,
temperature skyrocketed,
acid rained from the sky,
everything died:
the most massive extinction
in recorded history.
All those fossils,
oil now. Of course.

I was born here,
to the pasture,
spiny mesquites,
cracked red earth.
I imagined being born underwater,
born a suggestion

of what's to come,
something so basic
it could survive
when earth starts over,
a nautilus, maybe,
all tentacles, no memory.

I dreamed of it, the sea
before its horrific death,
before millions of years
sun blazed over lifeless desert.
Sometimes, waking I thought
I heard the waves.

Nautilus

Lucifer at the Tea Party

My mother will tell you about reading the invitation to me—
Hannah Miller's 4th birthday, a dress-up party—
the way I said, *Oh good, I'll wear my devil costume,*
how she explained that's not at all what they meant.
Think tea party. Think fancy.

Oh, I said. *Then I'm not going.*

When Hannah's mother asked me at preschool pickup
if I was planning to attend,
my mother explained the misunderstanding
after I said, *Nope.*
Oh, Hannah's mother said,
just bring her in whatever she wants to wear.

I don't believe I remember this.
Isn't it strange? The way story blurs
with memory, the sweet mythology
we make of ourselves.

Ask my mother and she will show you the photo:
little girls clad in lace, sashes, tiny gloves,
sitting in a circle, heads bent
as Hannah opens a gift,
and me, kneeling in the background,

dark eyes looking square at the camera,

my horns crooked, the hellfire on my red, red cape

just visible at the edge of the frame.

Elementary

My fourth grade teacher told me
she dreamt I belonged to her:
together we traveled by boat.
I imagined the unending sea,
my young teacher squinting in sunlight,
a life with another mother.

The day I had to explain
why I chased Rebekah Jones across the blacktop,
punched her in the back so hard she fell
and bloodied her skinny knees,
I really thought I was in trouble.

You know that thing boys have
that girls don't? I said.
My teacher nodded.
She said I have one of those.

Before I could say sorry,
my teacher hugged me;
her sea-green eyes brimmed with tears.
I stood stunned through Rebekah's stiff apology.
Back at our desks,
she picked at the bandages on her knees;
I drew a series of boats.

Dream in Which I Am Wile E. Coyote

I am *Carnivorous vulgaris,*
Famishus famishus, other fake
Latin terms for *hungry,*

all ribs and red-rimmed
yellow eyes. I know
only one desire.

My desert is vacant
apart from the roadrunner.
I am forever chasing,
wielding knife and fork, down highways
disappearing into orange horizon.
Every time I get close,
the music swells.

I think ACME can save me,
a better blueprint
could tip the topsy
turvy laws of physics
in my favor. I imagine
picking my long, sharp teeth
with a purple feather.

I know

there is no death here.
I plummet from cliffs, crush
myself with anvils, explode
and explode and explode and still
live to paint the next
perfect railway tunnel.

The train is always coming.

That blasted *meep-meep*
echos in the rust-red canyon.
I am strapped to a rocket.
I am lighting the fuse.

Practice

I fought the urge to stop at the edge of the light.
I didn't want to seem chicken—teammates had vanished
into the dense dark of the desert after a soccer ball countless times—
they always made it back.

The first footfall that crunched mesquite branches under cleats
slowed me to a jog. I glanced back, reassured
by the humming dome of light enveloping the field,
the shrinking figures of the other girls.

A noise like paper shuffling
made me reckon the ball hit a yucca.
I guessed at how far out, stood still,
squinted into the low, spiky shadows,
listened for the coyote calls
that always gave the family dog
that grave look.

I remembered the day my mother
crushed a scorpion bearing
her whole brood on her back
in our formal living room,
the exodus of tarantulas
across highways before rain.
I prayed.

Relief swelled into my throat
as I spotted the ball, seized it, and fled.
From the safety of the field,
I faced the black expanse,
ground indistinguishable from sky,
stars and oil rigs gleaming.

Scorpion

Rules

They say sit like
a lady, stand up
straight. They say
boy or girl; heaven
or hell; the Lord
taketh away. They
say tomboy like
bless her heart
like prayer request like
she doesn't know
what's good. Say
sin; say sorry;
say you were
wrong. They say
no means no; they tell
so many lies. They
say be a good
girl, don't
say a word.

Misdirection

The first time I broke
a disposable razor, I accidentally
slashed my thumb.
I did not cry out.
I freed the single, flimsy blade.
My intentional work
came out neater, bled less.

I was twelve and knew my body
was haunted. I slid the blade
between dictionary pages,
returned the volume to my bookshelf.
This is how I learned to hide in the open.

My inner thighs were so
easily unseen,
even in the locker room,
in department store fitting rooms with my mother.
I learned to create distractions,
to stand at the perfect angle. I knew
people cannot see
what they are not looking for.

Chaparral

They say X-shaped tracks belong to the roadrunner.
Can't tell if she's coming or going; she misleads evil spirits.
They say the bird will guide a lost person to road.

Most things fear the diamondback. Venom is absolute.
Roadrunner full tilt, slim brown and gold body
parallel to the ground; she hears the rattle,
stops still.

Coiled, fangs ready;
wings kick up a dust cloud;
the snake strikes—
one misfire then
another and another—
beak snaps shut
square between those black eyes.
Bird bashes reptile skull over rocks,
narrow neck extending
full height with each blow,
shatters bone—

easier to swallow that way.

Roadrunner

Rainmakers, 1891

Eighteen months and not so much
as a spit of rain. Dirt stained
the horizon red; tumbleweeds
lined fences around scorched fields.

They say war makes the rain.
Day and night, the boys
tore at the sky, counted
the government's dimes. No more
hand-wringing, no more prayer.
They flew bomb balloons, dynamite kites,
shoved explosives down prairie dog holes,
cannons reported in heaven.

The engineer would happily
show his letters, austere
signatures of all the decorated
officers you please—they told it the same—
raging battle then invariably violent rain.

The last balloon blossomed
into a globe of fire, illuminated
every object for miles—then
several dark seconds,
silent and open as the mouths of onlookers—

the inevitable crack, concussion,
birds taking flight and somehow
distant lightning.

Family Dog

She could see in the dark.
She slept when the pack slept,
knew more about
the creatures in the yard
than I could stomach.
I have such an indoor life,
such tender feet, I cannot
hear the thunder
'til it's above me.
She was the sweetest thing
to ever kill and eat a bird.
I walked her
every evening and thought
if there is such thing
as freedom
I will never know it

Corgi

II

Warbirds

Ninth grade field trip, Commemorative Air Force:
we filed through the collection of WWII nose art,
massive painted pinup girls on jagged-edge metal,
like torn pages of a dirty magazine.
Boys behind me shoved and snickered,
called each other *fag*.
I squinted up at cartoonish women,
the perfect Os of their mouths,
heart-shaped bottoms, bare breasts.
They were more bizarre than alluring,
accompanied by slogans for sex or death like
Target for Tonight or
Just Once More.
In the next room, we saw
replicas of Fat Man and Little Boy suspended,
mid-drop, surrounded by photos of mushroom clouds.
How strange, I thought, to go into battle this way,
such sweet phrases for devastation.

Education

I signed the abstinence agreement readily.
God, they're right, I thought,
still startled by the explicit images—
bodies infested, gaping pustules—
on handouts they said I should keep.
Sixteen and all
bones, unbloomed,
I knew stubble
and clumsy hands, the urgency
a boy will press to your thigh.
I knew what happens to girls like me.
I stood in the long line
in the high school library,
my peers shifted and sighed,
each of them signed contracts
that bound our bodies
to purity—the only way
to feel safe.

Close

A battle of the bands in a Christian coffee shop:
interchangeable skinny boys in church camp T-shirts
clinging to guitars. Everyone was there.

Bored, my best friend Rachel and I left.
Together we stood at the intersection
facing the yellowed glow of the convenience store.
I stepped off the curb as the signal clicked: Walk.
I took two strides

then a truck roared through the red light—

she yanked me back—

the side mirror
swiped my breath,
my shirt whipped against my skin.

I turned to her wide eyes, her open mouth;
she dropped her grip on my arm and said,
I think you owe me your life now, right?
I counted five fingertip bruises
among my blessings.

Transmission

You have to get the ratio right, Dad's voice clear
despite frustration. *Ease off that clutch,*
give 'er some gas—damn!

The eighteenth time the car heaved
its bucking death rattle, it was decided
my mother should teach me.

You can feel it, she said. *You're just going to know.*

How? I cranked the ignition again
and again, *What am I supposed to feel?*

Windows down, shoes off,
the mercy of the A/C silenced—

Just listen.

I longed for the shade of bleachers
on the far side of the sweltering stadium parking lot.

I inhaled, drew back on the clutch,
let the rising hum of gas to engine vibrate
inside my ribs, the car rolled, coughed once,
gained wonderful momentum until

I felt the strain, the need
for release and without thinking

hit second gear.

Observation

One winter I dated a boy
in a letterman jacket
from the one-gas-station town
down the road. Peter drove
a jacked-up Suburban equipped
with a high-powered spotlight,
night vision goggles stashed
under the driver's seat.
He claimed expertise
at interrupting couples parking
and playing cops and robbers.
I was always up for a game.
I never advised against
off-roading, never asked him
to slow down. One day he noticed
the knife in my pocket and said,
You know, sweetheart, you always were
a bit different.

Crush

Every day after third period she smiled at me.
I'd spend fourth period picturing
her reading, brushing her teeth,
shopping for the blackest hair dye on the shelf.
·I felt sure it had a name like abyss.
I imagined her delighted, thinking
Yes, this is dark enough.

Eventually, I told her my name,
that my daydreams never
included boys. Tabitha started
driving me to lunch sometimes,
always used every available condiment,
opened herself to any flavor.
Why not? she'd say.

The first time she put her hand on my knee
she felt a tremble roll through me,
heard my breath stop. *I know*
I make you nervous, she said, squeezing.
I was next to her on a stool in an empty café,
the barista leaning in the alley with a cigarette.

That day she showed me her room:
blackout curtains and burned-down candles,

books stacked in the corner—
every inch of what I dreamed.
I didn't have to say it.

I would, she said,
believe me. It's just
my boyfriend would be mad.

Santa Rita, 1921

Frank Pickrell checked his pocket for the envelope

as he looked up at the derrick, stark

against clear West Texas sky.

He had no experience in oil

but plenty friends, some of them savvy enough

to convince New York Catholic nuns to buy in.

He figured the nuns had never seen a thing like this.

He recalled a roughneck joking:

Ain't got but one road. All you hear

is roadrunners, rattlers, and rig cranking away.

Women of faith, skeptical about their investment,

told Frank the rose sealed in the envelope was blessed,

made him promise he'd climb to the top

and name the well for the patron saint of impossible things.

He scaled the derrick, mouthing words they gave him.

At the top, he tore open the envelope,

said *I hereby christen thee*

Santa Rita as dry red petals caught the wind.

Santa Rita No.1

Study

Knocking on Sarah's door was never easy.
Her mother wasn't sure what sort of girl I was.
She'd peer over her glasses, touch the cross
hanging at her chest. The dread that woman would answer
sat like a stone in my mouth.

Sarah would fling open the door, hug me
with such lack of hesitation I'd forget to be afraid.

Thursdays we did calculus together,
side by side on an oversized couch.
She never asked before
she slid her cold feet under my leg.
I tried my best to be warm.
She was brilliant and I was bright enough,
curious, at least, to know the how-much of things.
She leaned close as she compared my tiny, precise
numbers and symbols to the careful curves of her own.

I'd notice the smells of fresh baking before
I'd see her mother standing there,
with a plate of cookies still too hot to touch, two glasses of milk,
a wide, unmoving smile.

Prelude

Hard to believe Leah had lived in this town
all of her sixteen years and hadn't seen the used bookstore.
You had to know it to find it,
downtown behind the old pharmacy with the soda counter.

There were no other patrons, only a man
behind the counter reading a fat paperback.
We chose different entries into the labyrinth of shelves.
I moved quietly, stopping to touch spines of rare books,
listening for her footsteps.
I never let her get too far from me.

Hey! she said, as she popped around the corner,
You gotta see this. She took my wrist, led me
into the romance section, pointed at the row of covers.
Look, she said, *they're all the same.*

Each cover displayed couples embracing,
their open mouths trapped in the instant
just before the kiss. I remembered last summer,
the playground at night, how she stood
so close to me, how my breath stopped
when she looked at me, how she looked away.

Let's look for a cover where they're actually kissing, she said.
We searched every shelf together and didn't find a single one.

Boyfriend

I liked dating Joseph well enough.
He had a car, he was punctual,
memorized my locker combination,
left me notes, drawings, flowers.

He said *I love you* so easily. His sweet,
open face never questioned me,
even when I pulled away, even when
I didn't say it back.

Alone in his bedroom, I felt
his weight, his hands, tension
rippling under his skin.
He was not shy in wanting, but never
asked for anything: *Holding you is enough.*

Once, lying next to him, he reached for my hip
to pull me closer, and for a split second,
I thought he was going for my belt.
I sat up so quick
my forehead cracked him square in the nose.
Stunned by a bright flash of pain,
I blinked until he came back into focus.

Both hands covering his face, he turned away.
Are you okay? I said, touching his shoulder.
He faced me, red gushing between his fingers:
It's a good thing I love you.

Horned Toad

The horned toad is disappearing
but I have seen them:
sharp scales, crown of horns,
desert devil queen.
She'll let you pick her up,
sit docile in your hand.
She knows what'll eat a lizard
and what won't.

Nobody hides like her:
she's mastered the art of stillness,
wears impeccable camouflage,
buries herself in the dirt.
Nobody fights like her:
she puffs up to twice her size,
daring a predator to swallow
a body of blades.
She saves her most spectacular weapon
for coyotes and foxes—the threat
makes blood swell into her head,
erupt from her eyes;
she aims the stream directly into a fanged mouth.
It tastes so foul they run from her.

Though she predates humans by millions of years,

she recedes farther into desert as home turns
golf course, strip mall, subdivision, parking lot.
If you're sharp enough, you might see her
basking on some lonesome road
or devouring harvester ants in a mesquite pasture,
but don't be surprised
if you never do.

Horned
Lizard

Flurry

I couldn't remember the last time I saw snow.
My white-tipped yard looked like the endless bloom
of cotton fields flanking the highway to Lubbock.

Rachel grabbed her coat as I got my camera.
I was not a great photographer,
evidenced by a box full of pictures
that didn't turn out how I imagined.
That night I got a keeper:

her upturned palms, her white coat,
the black night around her
starred with snowflakes,
her unmistakable joy.

Unsupervised

I had no real desire to follow rules,

just never much chance to break them.

I drank whatever the soccer girls handed me,

made a mental list of things to do

after they taught me *Never Have I Ever*

and I didn't lose a single round.

Warm-bellied and dizzy, I ambled arm-in-arm

through the house with my most sharp-tongued teammate,

now cheerful and open to suggestion.

Together, we recited the Ten Commandments

from a plaque on the wall,

laughter breaking every *Thou shalt not.*

On the back porch, the goalkeeper told me stories:

other sins, other parentless nights.

Her voice, so powerful during games,

was hushed and sweet. She tried

to blow smoke rings with a cigar.

I watched each lazy U

dissipate in the porch light.

She asked, *Can you keep secrets?*

and I swore I could.

Proximity

I sat alone on the soccer bus,
alternating window and aisle, unsure
if I was lucky or lonely.

I loved the game. I was never safer
than in uniform, indistinguishable
from other girls at a distance.
I loved bus rides even better.
On the way, I savored anticipation.
On the dark journey home,
I never slept like the others.
I kept the quiet for them.

I was startled when Chloe Williams draped across my lap,
ignoring the empty seat next to me.
She was a senior with an attitude
and a knack for never being open on the field.

What do you fantasize about? she breathed,
so close her lips grazed my ear.

I don't have much of an imagination, I said.

She put her hand on my cheek,
directed my gaze into her own.

Oh, I doubt that, she said. *I bet there are a few things
that could make you wet.*

I didn't turn to watch her walk away.
The sudden absence of her weight was at once
empty and promising. I scanned the faces
of my sleeping teammates and knew—no one saw.

Confession

No one needs to know a secret
to sense its weight. Who knew
what sort of girl I was, anyway?
I couldn't answer
the most basic questions: *Do you know*
where you'll go when you die?
Do you know who saved you?

David figured I wouldn't tell a soul,
pinned me to the couch in my father's den,
pressed my hand against
his insistent threat—
I did that sort of thing,
right?

He was Sarah's on-again/off-again;
she thought she knew him.
Easy to buy that country-boy routine:
the drawl, the manners, his perfect
attendance at Sunday school.

Crying over calculus homework,
my solutions blurred as I tried
to tell her, *Don't be alone with him*
ever again, please, please.

As my throat tightened,
her eyes narrowed. She knew
any heathen will lie;
some women
only ruin a man.
I remembered the framed photo
in her bedroom: his sleepy smile,
his arm around her shoulder.
I'll pray for you, she said.

Camera Shy

My junior prom date was in one photo.
Fellow misfit cleaned up nice, Josh stood
stiffly next to me in my parents' foyer.
He didn't have his arm around me.

He was inexplicably furious
before we could even order dinner,
started pacing and cursing, and I,
despite my braces, my borrowed dress,
the truly unfortunate miscommunication
that resulted in my present haircut,
I was going to have fun, with or without him.

My year had been glorious, rich with pretty friends—
they'd done everything to convince me:
found me the dress, introduced me to him,
and tonight, they did not disappoint.
The photos caught them laughing, luminous,
linked arm in arm with me, showing off
sparkly shoes and complicated updos.
My posture told everyone
I'd never worn a strapless dress before.
They said I looked beautiful
and I believed them.

Ducking my date as a slow dance came on,
I was surprised to feel someone clasp my hand—

Dance with me—

and then, in my arms, Angel Aporongao, the Filipina girl in all my classes,
whose name I savored syllable by sweet syllable every time
she corrected the tortuous tongues of substitute teachers.

She swayed close to me, the baby's breath in her hair brushed my
cheek.
I almost didn't hear the clowny boy in the lime-green vest
gasp dramatically as he pointed at us;
she laughed, tossed him her camera and said,
Don't just stare, take a picture.

As the flash went off
I felt myself
stand up straight.

Grey Fox

As earth swallows sun, the fox
quickens. She knows darkness
wakes the pack. Coyote
is not brother. Blood
is only blood.

The fox hears the jackrabbit
tremble, knows how many
fill her belly. The pack stirs.
Hunger knows only itself.

Grey Fox

Trigger

This, Caleb said, *is a single-action*
semiautomatic, as he leveled
a pistol to my face. *That means*
the trigger only does one thing.

The dim light of his bedroom gleamed
on the barrel, close enough
I could smell grease.
I thought back
to idling in his driveway

past curfew, gripping
the steering wheel as he said
But I love you
and I said *Just friends.*
I remembered the slam
of the car door as the deafening

click of the hammer thundered
through my chest. He smiled,
tossed the gun in the air
and caught it on the flat of his hand.
He winked as he resumed
pointing it at me.

I heard my own cruel
laughter. He dropped
his smile as I said,
You wouldn't
you fucking
pansy. A tomboy
knows bravado works
better than surrender.

He put the gun down on the bed.
As I left I imagined
his high-thread-count sheets,
metal still warm
from his hands.

III

Laws

1. *A body at rest tends to stay at rest; a body in motion tends to stay in motion.*

My sigh steamed in the frigid morning;
the sky was the same color as the parking lot
and I had a physics test to study for.

I liked school better this early.
The quiet gave way to my footfalls,
the equations I murmured like psalms.
The library waited for me.

2. *Acceleration is proportional to the magnitude of the imposed force.*

I saw the truck take the corner,
rattle down the street as I stepped
onto the crosswalk. It slowed as it approached.

I regarded the driver, a blond boy
I'd known since middle school.
I was square in front of his hood ornament
when his eyes narrowed
and I knew—

Dyke! he yelled over the engine's sudden roar
as the truck surged forward—

I dodged, barely—

my physics book slapped pavement,
fluttered open.

3. *For every action there is an equal and opposite reaction.*

His rumbling laughter receded.
I picked up my book. I found
the library empty.

Rumors

I quit changing in the track locker room
the third time half the girls walked out
when I walked in.

One day I exited the restroom stall
to find the head cheerleader
rearranging her dark cascade of curls.
Oh, have you heard? she said,
Apparently I'm pregnant.

I heard many things.
Her life in hearsay was drunken,
wild, sometimes alarming.

Well, apparently I'm gay, I said.

She turned, looked exactly
at my face and said, *We should switch.*

I laughed. She accepted
my handshake, squeezed
a little harder as she said, *Good.*

Shipwreck

In history, I learned about explorers:
fleets of ships, grossly inaccurate maps,
successes and debts, naming everything for kings.

My teacher told us all about *La Belle*,
the French ship wrecked
off the Texas Gulf coast in 1686,
how they unearthed the whole thing in 1995
from the sludge of Matagorda Bay.
It was extraordinary, she said,
truly an archeological feat.

This is what I remember:
a survivor's journal reported
the crew was stranded,
dehydrated, starving,
denied supplies by their drunken pilot.
They were warned
not to eat the cactuses.
A desperate man greedily shoved
a whole prickly pear in his mouth.
He couldn't have known
about the invisible spines,
how they would lodge in his throat,

how quick the swelling,
how slow the suffocation.

Remember: I love the surprise
of yellow flowers, red fruit
ripening purple, the fact that
some beautiful things
should never be touched.

Prickly Pear

Well-Mannered Girls

Fine, I'll show you, Lily said,
extracting a garment bag from her closet.
Inside, a perfectly white formal dress I recognized
from the portrait of her sister in the hall.
My closet never contained such a thing.

You really are a debutante, I said.

A belle, she corrected. *Fucking absurd.*
Mother just adores the little white gloves.
I marveled at her precise articulation of crude syllables,
clarity gained from voice lessons.

I imagined her at the Belle Ball,
on the arm of a black tux. I knew
she'd wish he could be me.
Wouldn't her mother
just *adore* that?

She pulled me to my feet, curtsied,
placed my hand on her waist.
Step. Together. Laughing, *Don't lead.*
I focused on my shoes. *Step.*
Together. Look at me. There,
see? Now you got it.

Illumination

You can't watch me, Lily said.
Next to her on the piano bench
I could smell her hair.
Okay, I said, *Where should I go?*

She directed me to lie down on the couch;
with her back to me, she could pretend to be alone.
I stared at the high ceiling of her living room
while she cursed through two false starts.
I shut my eyes and waited.

The mournful melody tripped at first.
I recognized it from *Romeo & Juliet*.
I almost felt her take that deep breath
just before the room filled with her voice;
its surprising clarity swelled
into my chest, rang sweetly in my bones.

I sat up, almost involuntarily, peeked over the couch
to watch: her impeccable posture, the slow
sway of her body, her certain hands.

I never guessed that her promise to sing for me
would be a gift, that she could possess such light,
that she could show it to me.

Flash Floods

After I kissed Lily
it rained for three days.
Roads swelled into rivers,
as they do in towns built thinking
flood isn't coming.

Out my window, the broad
face of the STOP sign whipped
back and forth, frantic, as if
checking over one shoulder,
then the other.

For three nights I dreamed
sea monsters, shipwrecks;
I woke salt-stung, lungs
bursting, sheets twisted tentacles.

On the fourth night, she parked
down the block from my house,
waited on the sidewalk,
avoiding the streetlight reflected
on puddled pavement.

I slipped out the door so quiet
she didn't hear. Approaching

her dark figure, I did not know
the content of her nightmares,
what kind of secrets she could carry.
I only knew she would kiss me.

Laura Welch, 1963

You know, Laura never could see too good.
They really ought to do something
about that road. It's black as anything
out there at night. Those girls just wanted
to see the show at the drive-in.
Did you hear it was only two days
after Laura's 17th birthday?
Shame, you know, that boy
had a whole life ahead of him;
football star and all, he sure made
a fine Lee Rebel.

Folks in that neighborhood
off Big Spring Street could *hear* the crash.
Can you imagine?

Oh, she was pretty banged up;
thrown from her daddy's Impala,
black eyes, ankle broke. Not dead, though;
the boy was the only one. They say
his mama hasn't quit crying since.

Laura never said a word about it.
Didn't go to the funeral, nothing.
The school got that Confederate cannon

as a memorial. You know,
those kids nominated Laura
to homecoming court.
Bless her heart.

Flood Gauge

I'd never fought with Lily before.
When I got into her SUV, I matched
her steely silence; I was plenty
pissed and not about to back down.

I recognized the road;
when she turned streetlights dissipated.
SLOW DOWN signs
glared in pitch-blackness.
She picked up speed, the road ahead
dipped into the draw.
No point building a bridge
if the creek won't rise.

She hit the gas harder; I clutched
door handle into downslope,
bumper sparked pavement,
the flash of the roadside flood gauge
clear as I imagined
any final image would be.
Upslope, for a split second
we were weightless,
then impact, fishtail,
control.

She didn't look at me,
didn't flinch or smile or speak.
She drove me home,
pulled up to my house
and kissed me.

Lily

I couldn't have known.
She had perfect
teeth, a four-post bed
with a dreamy canopy,
she showed me

photos from around the world,
that model smile with so many
postcard backdrops,
her father's name
on a building downtown.
She talked to me on the phone
late at night, slipped into French
as she drifted off.

The obnoxious quarterback
called me *faggot* in the parking lot
and she dared him, *Come closer
and say that again.*

The first time she hurt me,
I thought *accident*. I leaned
into my bathroom mirror,
counted her perfect teeth in the deep
bruise on my collarbone.
I hid it.

The first time she threatened me
was in a love letter, a full paragraph
for how she would hunt me,
beat me, bleed me if I ever left,
slipped between passages
of fevered praise, *I adore you*
you're beautiful
come closer.

The first time I dared
to leave, she turned up
everywhere. I rounded
the corner in the bookstore
and there she was with that smile.
I flashed back to how calm
she seemed as her hands
tightened around my neck,
how I tried to look her in the eye
as everything went still, my vision
narrowing into blackness,
the throbbing in my ears growing
distant. I steadied myself against a bookcase,
scanned the store for someone I knew;
no luck.

At school, the assistant principal glared at me,

said, *You hug your friends*

a bit too long; one day some boys

followed me home, fired a pellet gun

through my open window at a stoplight,

called me *dyke* as every pop

stung my cheeks; the way my father

said *queer* tasted like blood in my mouth;

my mother said, *Those people*

should never have children. I spent

weeks finding pellets rolling

in my floorboard. Lily said,

No one else

will ever love you.

Monday in December

I shivered in the dark Starbucks parking lot,
waiting for Lily to pick me up.
I glanced through the foggy window at my friends,
warm and laughing over festive cups.
They knew they were my alibi
but hadn't seen the bruises around my neck,
hadn't traced her fingers in them.
I considered how winter is kind in that way.
The scarf I bought was so pretty.

When I got into her SUV,
I noticed the back seat folded down.
She drove to her grandmother's vacant home
on the north side of town,
all the neighbors with horse stables.
She parked in the darkened driveway,
climbed into the back and I followed.

It takes a long time to take off
a pair of high-top Converse All Stars,
especially when they're laced
all the way up, double knotted,
just to be sure.

I'm going to think
about her slowly

loosening the laces,
the *thunk thunk* as they landed
near the spare tire.

I'm going to think
about all the things
a person could say in that time,
how I said nothing,
how I learned
she hurt me less
when I didn't struggle.

I'm going to tell myself
I don't remember what followed
and that will be partially true.
Each frame of this night will tick
perfectly through my mind
but I will not feel it.
For years, I will not
feel anything.

In two days, she's going to say
I know I raped you,
and I am not going to argue.

But then, I was back in her passenger seat,
tightening the laces on my All Stars,
double knot just
to be sure. She took me
back to my friends, my car,
the frigid Starbucks parking lot.
I looked at her, the passing streetlight
shadows across her still, blank face.
Somehow, I erupted
with laughter, hysterical,
rib-splitting. She said nothing
while I laughed like that
all the way there.

Shotgun

Rachel and I just drove,
knew every parking lot and pasture,
every copless stretch of highway.
I couldn't imagine
what kids in other towns did at night.

I earned permanent shotgun.
The other girls stopped trying
to call it even though no one
likes the backseat of a Mustang.
She laughed louder than the radio,
gunned it at yellow lights,
loved 24-hour drive-throughs
and fountain drinks.
The night after everything
went straight to hell

she picked me up,
hit 100 on the highway
but didn't ask questions,
cranked the music and let me cry.
The road was pitch-black, just stars
and the glint of reflectors
separating lanes.

She said *I love this song*
and we both sang.

Scharbauer Hotel, 1973

Day 1: October 28

After forty-five years of nooners and wheeler-dealers,
it came to this: fifteen thousand onlookers
on a Sunday morning ready for demolition.
Cheers erupted after dynamite blasts.
When the dust cleared, a wave of shock:
the hotel stood proud as ever.
That's what you call class.

Day 2: October 29

They brought on the oil field riggers;
bulldozers and explosives were futile.
She may not have been a moneymaker, but she sure
drew a crowd. They were rooting for her,
stubborn as hell, standing her ground.

Day 3: October 30

Cables snapped, equipment buckled,
a wrecking ball swinging again
and again and damn
if she wasn't still there.

Day 4: October 31

By then, she was weaving
about six inches with every pull.
Folks said it was a damn shame.
She'd be a pile of rubble
by day's end, you better believe it.

Injury

I wish I could remember how my rib broke.
Could I ask Lily?
Would she fill blanks in my memory with lies?

This is what I know:
the sun was up when I arrived
and down when I left;
the moments between are lost,
ink-black and muted in my mind.
I got into my car,
reached for my seat belt,
felt myself split, my breath
strangled by absolute pain.
I couldn't even cry out.

This is what I know:
nothing mends a broken rib but time.
I couldn't fill my lungs,
couldn't laugh or hug or sneeze
or run or reach for anything.
Childhood mishaps
were not education enough.
That time I plummeted
a good 30 feet from a tree,
that time a woman in a sedan

knocked me off my bike
and kept right on driving,
that was nothing, not even
close to the volume of suffering
a body can hold.

Lily told me she heard it snap.
She said this like she'd say
anything else, like weather
or homework, like accident
or coincidence. I was almost
jealous she knew what happened
but then again
maybe not.

Coyote

Driving downtown with my mother,
I saw a coyote lope over a crosswalk,
golden in broad daylight,
tongue lolling in the heat.

I learned legends in school,
coyote as trickster or god.
My father told me
folks hate them,
been trying to thin them out
for decades with all manner
of torture—poison, traps,
rifles in helicopters—but
they just adapt.
Kill them and they just
keep coming.

This is what I know:
they'll care for an injured mate
'til death; they live on cottontails
but pressured, they'll take a sheep;
it's not a good idea to leave a small pet
out at night; they're the only
creature to thrive like this,
desert turning concrete,

hunters always
coming. Listen. As sunset
dissolves to darkness
you can hear them.

Coyote

Volition

You never answered—
would it be weird?

I'd willfully forgotten the question.

The tour of Lily's empty house
was an excellent distraction.

She led me from one cavernous room
to the next, lush with claw-foot furniture,
endless bookshelves, pillows with gold tassels.

In the upstairs closet, I helped her
push a large box to reveal the crawlspace door.
She kneeled, slid the wood panel aside.

You can go in if you want.

I eased my way into the darkness,
past the surprisingly detailed Death Star
she or her brothers left there.
Folding knees to chest, I felt
jeans press against wounds
on my inner thigh, felt my shin bones
dig into bruises on my wrists.

She peered in at me, haloed
by the closet light.

Would it be weird if I wanted
to call you my girlfriend?

IV

Scorcher

Summer meant sweltering sidewalks,
the dog's forever-drooping tongue,
parched dusty lawns.
Rachel's aboveground pool
was nothing short of a blessing.

Once, heat hanging heavy past midnight,
she said, *Why don't we go skinny-dipping?*

Before I could say something chickenshit,
she shed her clothes, disappeared into dark water.
I scanned the windows of her sleeping house,
listened: only the rattle of cicadas.
I dropped my clothes and followed.

I gasped as the chill of water snapped through me.
She drifted a lazy circle, looked up
and said, *Damn, so many stars.*

It was so dark she was only illuminated
by moonlight on her shoulders.
I remembered that time in her room
she modeled new clothes for me,
spinning, striking poses, pleased
with my approval. I kept thinking

I should turn away
as she redressed again and again.
She never asked me to.

Now, enveloped in cool, merciful
water, in night magnificent with stars,
my body was not a secret anymore.

Supernova

Leah asked for stars so I drove
past the end of the roads where
mesquite trees narrowed the caliche path.

My headlights illuminated stark angles of cactuses,
glinted in wide eyes of some lone creature—a fox?
I killed the engine and desert concealed us
in abiding darkness.
Windows down, together
we faced the galaxy,
resplendent, at once immediate
and impossibly distant.

All evening, in rooms full of strangers,
her easy laughter chased
emptiness from my chest.
Now, alone, I mirrored
the stillness of her starlit face,
partook of her silence,
gave thanks in the vast cathedral of night.

AP English

There's no solid description of Grendel,
but I could imagine
his swampy musk, his breath hot
with rage, drawn from darkness
toward Herot, all the men singing,
their voices thick with mead.
I also know what joy sounds like
when it can never belong to you.

My teacher said monsters
make heroes but I figured
I knew guys like Beowulf,
all talk and toothy smiles,
daredevil for glory.
He beat his chest, claimed
he wouldn't even need a weapon.
I hoped he'd get eaten.

My classmates celebrated
Grendel's severed arm swinging
bloody from the rafters.
Villains, teacher said,
are integral to the plot.

I'd never read a monster with a mother.
Grendel's mother is nameless

but her grief-ridden howl
haunted my dreams. Beowulf entered
her lair under the lake
and I was breathless, imagining
ethereal light and still water,
how her sorrow must have echoed there.
I knew she couldn't win in a story like this,
but I loved her for coming close.

Jessica, 2007

Her first interview ever
and the newsman said,
You don't remember, do you?

20 years ago, her mother
turned for only a moment—
the last time no one was looking—
and Jessica was just
gone.

Let's get a good look
at that baby we prayed for.

18 months old, 58 hours spent
22 feet down an 8-inch pipe.
The biggest media frenzy
since the *Challenger*: dusty West Texas
tiny on television screens, her little voice
singing proof of life while America
wrung its hands. Folded knees to chest,
down there long enough to sleep twice,
long enough for medical professionals to decide
if she were bleeding, she'd have died already.
Jessica saved by Midland's can-do attitude,
that downhome determination,

that skill for drilling earth.
They say she belongs to everyone now.

The ordeal didn't end
when you were rescued,
did it?

15 surgeries, 9 blood transfusions,
6 weeks in the hospital,
1 toe sacrificed to stop gangrene,
1 school library break-in by the media
to steal her yearbook photo, age 11.

Show us your scars.
Tell us why you keep them.

Jessica pushed her hair aside,
leaned into the camera.

Devil with Roots

The mesquite tree is merciless; it'll invade
any overgrazed land. Those two-inch thorns
stab cattle, spook horses. They say it's war.
Ranchers drag chains through fields,
spread noxious chemicals
that'll sting the nose and ruin soil.
Some just burn the whole godforsaken place.

Before long it comes back around.

It survives the inferno of summer,
the only green for miles, everything else
singed into yellow death. They say
those seed pods can wait
a good 40 years 'til conditions are right.
Disturb a new shoot and one trunk turns to many.
Lateral roots 50 feet in all directions;
tap root 175 feet down, far as it takes to hit water.
You can cut it but never deep enough;
it's always rising beneath the surface.

Lord knows you can't do nothin' about a leviathan.

Might as well build fences with it.
Send it through the chipper and get to grillin'.

Chew the coating off the beans;

it's sweet like candy mama wouldn't let you have.

Learn to enjoy its little white flowers.

They'll be here when you're long gone.

Mesquite Tree

Graduation

The local paper always featured a photo of someone—
anonymous citizens doing everyday things—
under the heading *You Ought to Be in Pictures.*

Nothing to write about? I thought,
thumbing past children playing in sprinklers,
a woman presenting a cherry pie in both hands.

The morning after graduation
my mother woke me, paper in hand.
There I was, cap and gown,
captioned *class cutup,*
captured playing rock paper scissors
with my brother in the stadium seats.

I'm holding scissors
and an incisive, determined glare.

My mother called the paper,
claimed me her daughter
and ordered a color 8x10 to frame for the mantel.

Graduation was not boring like I imagined—
the pomp, the circumstance,
all of it thrummed through me,
joyful, dizzying, final.

My brother taught me many things,
not least the art of losing,
besting me every time, at every competition
by skill or luck or charm.
He won rock paper scissors that day, 5 to 3.

Standing back from the mantel
my mother assessed the new arrangement:
my siblings and me at Christmas,
the dog my parents loved first, before children,
the neat row of graduation handshakes—
sister, brother, me—then me
wielding scissors, a split second from smirking.

You look happy, she said.
Well, I said, *he had paper.*

Alma Mater

Everyone got real proud during George W's time in office,

seeing as he claimed us home. Laura's really the one from here.

My high school library made a whole display of memorabilia:

her yearbooks, a vintage megaphone,

her framed senior photo all broad face and big hair.

I carefully took a yearbook from the display:

'62, Lee High's first. Looking for Laura Welch,

I thumbed past construction photos,

bones of buildings that contained me,

a concept sketch of the facade

I stared down every morning from the parking lot.

I scanned row on row of white faces,

flat tops and flipped bobs, Confederate flags at pep rallies,

the homecoming court posing in front of a stage backdrop

painted to look like an antebellum plantation house.

I'd learned some history—the Civil War ended 1865,

Midland was founded 1885,

Brown vs. Board of Education 1954—

but those facts wouldn't add up until much later.

Midland had some time after the '54 ruling

before the feds came for them,

as they came for many cities resisting desegregation.

What did Midland do? Built a new high school,

ignored all those hometown ranchers and oil barons

so they could name it Robert E. Lee.

They taught the band "Dixie."

W got reelected when I was in college.

I was taking Black History, reckoning

with how to see myself, my country, my home,

in light of everything previously left out of my education:

the Klan's desire to "preserve" America,

Emmett Till's mother and her public mourning,

the lynching and the lynching and the lynching.

I swallowed each wrenching story

like a jagged stone. I picked up

a newspaper, stared at a photo of George and Laura

posing with an endless row of white columns

in front of that White House and thought

God help us all.

Parting Gift

Leah slid into my passenger seat
and said *I've got something to show you.*
It was August and against all odds
it was raining, brutal afternoon swelter
lifting into darkened sky.
She directed me to a patch of woods
off the side of the road,
flanked by desperate yellow fields.

As I followed her on foot toward the trees,
I did not consider the empty dorm room
eight hours away that waited for me.

A draw separated the woods from the field.
She did not hesitate to cross on a fallen tree.
I stopped. She turned back. I looked at her,
the wilderness behind her
haunting and lovely, and I thought
if I tried to cross, I'd fall.
She held out her hand.
I took it.

She led me through pathless forest to a clearing.
We looked up at the domed canopy,
lush and sudden green, drumming with raindrops.

I kissed her
and she kissed me back.
She touched my face.
This was what they mean
when they say *falling,*
when they say *fireworks.*
This was every lie I was ever told
illuminated, everything they said
I couldn't have.
This was also goodbye.

She didn't say anything,
not a single damn thing.
It was August and I didn't feel the rain.

Tarantula Hawk Wasp

Her bumbling mate is harmless and unarmed,
her flight is clumsy, nectar-drunk.
Don't be fooled.
Heed the warning
of her wondrous blue-black body,
third-of-an-inch stinger,
sienna wings.
Her venom blinds,
a lightning strike,
pain beyond imagination,
even for a creature big as you.

The tarantula knows
escape is the only defense.
Mother wasp will chase him from his burrow,
puncture, poison, paralyze,
drag him back to his home-now-tomb.
She'll place a single egg in the chamber,
select male or female offspring,
saving the largest spiders
for her voracious daughters.
She shuts the burrow when she leaves.

For 20 days her child feeds
on her helpless, living host,

swelling, quickening, saving
vital organs for last.

She emerges, slick
and thirsting for nectar.
She'll spend her days
wheeling around flowers,
avoiding her lone challenger—
the quick beak of the chaparral.

Can you imagine?
The ability to choose
your heirs, name
your single threat,
know everything
you will hunger for.

Tarantula
Hawk Wasp

Devil's Waterhole

This camping trip with Rachel was the last thing we'd do
before college separated us.
I couldn't wait to see the Devil's Waterhole.
They say Lucifer dwells beneath the surface.
We waded in, looked up at boys hollering
as they jumped into the water
from higher and higher on a pink granite cliff.

Let's do it, Rachel said, *Let's jump.*

I was stunned by the view from the top:
impossible expanse of sky over dense forest,
a hawk wheeling in the distance.
Rachel took a single deep breath then
leapt, plummeted so fast she struck the water
before I could think, *Wait.*
I scanned the surface, frantic
as ripples calmed
and she didn't come up.

Oh god.

Finally she burst from beneath,
already laughing.
You okay? I called. *Yeah!* she said,
You can do it!

I peered down at the jagged cliff,
the watchful faces of people below.
I searched the horizon for the hawk
but it was gone.
I inhaled, held it in, then

jumped.

Hawk

Acknowledgments

I am grateful to the editors of the following publications, in which some of these poems first appeared:

The Boiler

Cactus Heart

Crab Fat Magazine

Easy Street

Glitterwolf

IndieFeed: Performance Poetry

Prime Number Magazine

Mad Swirl

Radar Poetry

Split Rock Review

Southern Poetry Anthology: Texas, Texas Review Press

Texas Poetry Calendar 2017, Dos Gatos Press

Texas Poetry Calendar 2019, Kallisto Gaia Press

Turn a Phrase

Weaving the Terrain, Dos Gatos Press

Thanks to everyone who listened to these poems or indulged my weird facts about desert creatures. I am especially grateful to poets Gayle Reaves-King, Tria Wood, and Megan Peak for their feedback and friendship. Thanks also to Stevie Edwards and Trinica Sampson for their professional editorial guidance. Thanks to friends whose brilliance helped make this book what it is: Nandra Perry, Megan Routh, Kendra Greene,

Peter Meilleur, Dani Quesenberry, and Lorelei Willett. I am tremendously grateful to the folks at Wildacres Retreat in North Carolina for the hospitality of their artist residency. My Dallas–Fort Worth poetry friends are too numerous to name, but I am grateful to know so many lovely people. Thanks to Deep Vellum and The Wild Detectives for making space for poets.

The sources I read or consulted for this project are also too numerous to name. But the following sources were essential: Jimmy Patterson, *A History of Character: the Story of Midland Texas* (2014); John Howard Griffin, *Land of the High Sky* (1959); Laura Bush, *Spoken from the Heart* (2010); Mike Cochran and John Lumpkin, *West Texas: A Portrait of Its People and Their Raw and Wondrous Land* (1999); Edward Powers, *War and the Weather* (1890); editor Laura McCullough, *A Sense of Regard: Essays on Poetry and Race* (2015); editors Claudia Rankine, Beth Loffreda, and Max King Cap, *The Racial Imaginary: Writers on Race in the Life of the Mind* (2015); Texas State Historical Association, *Handbook of Texas* and *Texas Almanac*; Texas Archeological Research Laboratory, *Texas Beyond History*; the Permian Basin Petroleum Museum; and countless court document and newspaper archives, especially those including the *Midland Reporter-Telegram*. Thanks also to every Midlander who answered my questions and shared their stories with me.

I am grateful to my family. I'm lucky y'all have always believed in my writing. Greatest thanks of all to my wife, Ashley, who has given me so many perfect things, including our daughter and all of the artwork in this book. Home is what you make it; thanks for always making it beautiful with me.

Thank you all
for your support.
We do this for you,
and could not do
it without you.

DEEP
VELLUM

PARTNERS

 pixel texel

 LIFE IN DEEP ELLUM

EMBREY FAMILY FOUNDATION

 COMMON DESK

ALLRED
CAPITAL MANAGEMENT
of
RAYMOND JAMES®

ADDITIONAL DONORS, CONT'D

Mark Haber
Mary Cline
Maynard Thomson
Michael Reklis
Mike Soto
Mokhtar Ramadan
Nikki & Dennis Gibson
Patrick Kukucka
Patrick Kutcher
Rev. Elizabeth & Neil Moseley
Richard Meyer

Scott & Katy Nimmons
Sherry Perry
Sydneyann Binion
Stephen Harding
Stephen Williamson
Susan Carp
Susan Ernst
Theater Jones
Tim Perttula
Tony Thomson

SUBSCRIBERS

Joseph Rebella
Michael Lighty
Shelby Vincent
Margaret Terwey
Ben Fountain

AVAILABLE NOW FROM DEEP VELLUM

MICHÈLE AUDIN · *One Hundred Twenty-One Days* · translated by Christiana Hills · FRANCE

BAE SUAH · *Recitation* · translated by Deborah Smith · SOUTH KOREA

MARIO BELLATIN · *Mrs. Murakami's Garden* · translated by Heather Cleary · MEXICO

EDUARDO BERTI · *The Imagined Land* · translated by Charlotte Coombe · ARGENTINA

CARMEN BOULLOSA · *Texas: The Great Theft* · *Before* · *Heavens on Earth*
translated by Samantha Schnee · Peter Bush · Shelby Vincent · MEXICO

MAGDA CARNECI · *FEM* · translated by Sean Cotter · ROMANIA

LEILA S. CHUDORI · *Home* · translated by John H. McGlynn · INDONESIA

MATHILDE CLARK · *Lone Star* · translated by Martin Aitken · DENMARK

SARAH CLEAVE, ed. · *Banthology: Stories from Banned Nations* ·
IRAN, IRAQ, LIBYA, SOMALIA, SUDAN, SYRIA & YEMEN

LOGEN CURE · *Welcome to Midland: Poems* · USA

ANANDA DEVI · *Eve Out of Her Ruins* · translated by Jeffrey Zuckerman · MAURITIUS

PETER DIMOCK · *Daybook from Sheep Meadow* · USA

CLAUDIA ULLOA DONOSO · *Little Bird*, translated by Lily Meyer · PERU/NORWAY

ROSS FARRAR · *Ross Sings Cheree & the Animated Dark: Poems* · USA

ALISA GANIEVA · *Bride and Groom* · *The Mountain and the Wall*
translated by Carol Apollonio · RUSSIA

FERNANDA GARCIA LAU · *Out of the Cage* · translated by Will Vanderhyden · ARGENTINA

ANNE GARRÉTA · *Sphinx* · *Not One Day* · *In/concrete* · translated by Emma Ramadan · FRANCE

JÓN GNARR · *The Indian* · *The Pirate* · *The Outlaw* · translated by Lytton Smith · ICELAND

GOETHE · *The Golden Goblet: Selected Poems* · *Faust, Part One*
translated by Zsuzsanna Ozsváth and Frederick Turner · GERMANY

NOEMI JAFFE · *What are the Blind Men Dreaming?* · translated by Julia Sanches & Ellen Elias-Bursac · BRAZIL

CLAUDIA SALAZAR JIMÉNEZ · *Blood of the Dawn* · translated by Elizabeth Bryer · PERU

PERGENTINO JOSÉ · *Red Ants* · MEXICO

TAISIA KITAISKAIA · *The Nightgown & Other Poems* · USA

JUNG YOUNG MOON · *Seven Samurai Swept Away in a River* · *Vaseline Buddha*
translated by Yewon Jung · SOUTH KOREA

KIM YIDEUM · *Blood Sisters* · translated by Ji yoon Lee · SOUTH KOREA

JOSEFINE KLOUGART · *Of Darkness* · translated by Martin Aitken · DENMARK

YANICK LAHENS · *Moonbath* · translated by Emily Gogolak · HAITI

FORTHCOMING FROM DEEP VELLUM

SHANE ANDERSON · *After the Oracle* · USA

MARIO BELLATIN · *Beauty Salon* · translated by David Shook · MEXICO

MIRCEA CĂRTĂRESCU · *Solenoid*
translated by Sean Cotter · ROMANIA

LEYLÂ ERBIL · *A Strange Woman*
translated by Nermin Menemencioğlu & Amy Marie Spangler· TURKEY

RADNA FABIAS · *Habitus* · translated by David Colmer · CURAÇAO/NETHERLANDS

SARA GOUDARZI · *The Almond in the Apricot* · USA

GYULA JENEI · *Always Different* · translated by Diana Senechal · HUNGARY

UZMA ASLAM KHAN • *The Miraculous True History of Nomi Ali* • PAKISTAN

SONG LIN · *The Gleaner Song: Selected Poems* · translated by Dong Li · CHINA

TEDI LÓPEZ MILLS · *The Book of Explanations* · translated by Robin Myers · MEXICO

JUNG YOUNG MOON · *Arriving in a Thick Fog*
translated by Mah Eunji and Jeffrey Karvonen · SOUTH KOREA

FISTON MWANZA MUJILA · *The Villain's Dance*, translated by Roland Glasser · *The River in the Belly: Selected Poems*, translated by Bret Maney · DEMOCRATIC REPUBLIC OF CONGO

LUDMILLA PETRUSHEVSKAYA · *Kidnapped: A Crime Story*, translated by Marian Schwartz · *The New Adventures of Helen: Magical Tales*, translated by Jane Bugaeva · RUSSIA

SERGIO PITOL · *The Love Parade* · translated by G. B. Henson · MEXICO

MANON STEFAN ROS · *The Blue Book of Nebo* · WALES

JIM SCHUTZE · *The Accommodation* · USA

SOPHIA TERAZAWA · *Winter Phoenix: Testimonies in Verse* · POLAND

BOB TRAMMELL · *The Origins of the Avant-Garde in Dallas & Other Stories* · USA

BENJAMIN VILLEGAS · *ELPASO: A Punk Story* · translated by Jay Noden · MEXICO